She Persisted

TEMPLE GRANDIN

—INSPIRED BY—

She Persisted

by Chelsea Clinton & Alexandra Boiger

. . . .

TEMPLE GRANDIN

. . . .

Written by
Lyn Miller-Lachmann

Interior illustrations by
Gillian Flint

PHILOMEL

PHILOMEL BOOKS
An imprint of Penguin Random House LLC, New York

First published in the United States of America by Philomel Books,
an imprint of Penguin Random House LLC, 2022

Visit us online at penguinrandomhouse.com.

Library of Congress Cataloging-in-Publication Data is available.

Printed in the United States of America

HC ISBN 9780593353530
10 9 8 7 6 5 4 3 2 1
PB ISBN 9780593353554
10 9 8 7 6 5 4 3 2 1

WOR

Edited by Jill Santopolo and Talia Benamy.
Design by Ellice M. Lee.
Text set in LTC Kennerley.

For Charlie

She
Persisted

....

DEAR READER,

As Sally Ride and Marian Wright Edelman both powerfully said, "You can't be what you can't see." When Sally said that, she meant that it was hard to dream of being an astronaut, like she was, or a doctor or an athlete or anything at all if you didn't see someone like you who already had lived that dream. She especially was talking about seeing women in jobs that historically were held by men.

I wrote the first *She Persisted* and the books that came after it because I wanted young girls—and children of all genders—to see women who worked hard to live their dreams. And I wanted all of us to see examples of persistence in the face of different challenges to help inspire us in our own lives.

I'm so thrilled now to partner with a sisterhood of writers to bring longer, more in-depth versions of stories of women's persistence and achievement to readers. I hope you enjoy these chapter books as much as I do and find them inspiring and empowering.

And remember: If anyone ever tells you no, if anyone ever says your voice isn't important or your dreams are too big, remember these women. They persisted and so should you.

Warmly,

Chelsea Clinton

TEMPLE GRANDIN

TABLE OF CONTENTS

....

....

On Her Own Schedule

Temple Grandin's mother loved her daughter very much. But when Temple was a baby, her mother, Eustacia, worried about her a lot too. Eustacia worried because Temple was unusually quiet. While her friends' babies babbled cheerfully, then spoke words and sentences, Temple stayed silent.

From the age of six months on, Temple stiffened when Eustacia held her. She hated it when people hugged her. She would scratch and kick "like a little wild animal."

Eustacia noticed that Temple often seemed to live in her own world. Growing up, she would sit on the beach and watch sand running through her fingers. At home, she liked to tear paper up

into strips or confetti and arrange it into piles. When Eustacia played the piano, Temple would rock or spin around in circles while humming to herself.

Temple's father didn't have much patience with children, especially with one who was different. He wanted to send her to a home for children with disabilities. But Eustacia refused to give up on her daughter.

Fortunately, the Grandins had a lot of money, and they lived in Boston, where there were many well-known universities and hospitals. Eustacia brought Temple to the doctors at Boston Children's Hospital. They tested Temple's hearing. It was normal. After more tests, they told Eustacia that Temple had brain damage. The doctors suggested that Temple go for speech therapy.

Many years later, Temple would learn she was autistic. Autistic people have brains that work differently. They can often focus intently on things that fascinate them, like how sand looks and feels when it runs through fingers. But they sometimes have a hard time communicating their thoughts and feelings, which is why Temple didn't speak and why she screamed in frustration instead.

In 1947, the year Temple was born, very few children were diagnosed as autistic, which means that lots of doctors didn't realize what was going on with their patients. Those who were diagnosed usually lived in bleak hospital-like institutions for people with disabilities. The doctor who defined autism in 1943, Leo Kanner, thought it was uncommon and believed that doctors could use a few specific signs to tell who was autistic. Even though

Kanner didn't have any recommendations for what to do about it then, doctors who read his work assumed the children he described could not live with their families or attend a regular school.

For more than a year after meeting with the doctors, Temple didn't say a word. Eustacia hired a nanny to play games with her so she would learn how to take turns, follow directions, and lose without throwing a tantrum. After Temple started speaking at age four, Eustacia taught her to read. They spent thirty minutes on reading lessons, five days a week, and Temple learned quickly. She showed her mother and everyone else that she would grow up and learn on her own schedule!

Eustacia's father, Temple's grandfather, John C. Purves, was a famous inventor who developed

the autopilot system for airplanes. With her mother and grandfather's encouragement, Temple used her imagination to make things too. She discovered her mother's sewing kit and her father's toolbox. She made models and dioramas that impressed her family. Then she took them apart and made new things.

Temple was proud of her creations, even when

they didn't work the way she expected. She later said, "If one of my projects failed, I would experiment for many hours until I got it to work." Her ability to focus on things that fascinated her led to her persistence, and she pursued goals even if they were difficult to achieve or if other people stood in the way. Autism presented challenges for her, but it also gave her a lot of what she needed to meet those challenges!

Soon Temple had two younger sisters and a younger brother. Eustacia kept all the children on a strict schedule. Temple thrived on this schedule. She liked having rules to follow and knowing what would happen at every minute of every day.

Though things were going better at home, Temple struggled in school. Her mother sent her to a private elementary school with small classes, and there, she had kind teachers. But the other children teased her because she was different. They called her "weirdo" and "tape recorder" because she spoke in a flat voice and repeated facts that interested her but didn't interest the other kids.

When Temple was in ninth grade, she threw a book at a classmate who kept teasing her. She had gotten into many fights already, and this was the last straw! The school kicked her out. In addition, her parents divorced after years of not getting along. All these changes upset Temple.

Eustacia wanted Temple to live at home and go to a regular school, but she was coming to realize that maybe a boarding school that specialized in teens who had trouble controlling their emotions would be a better place for Temple to learn and grow.

. . . .

CHAPTER 2

The Squeeze Machine

At the boarding school, Temple lived on campus and visited her family only for holidays. Her mother married Ben Cutler, a musician in New York City, and moved there with Temple's sisters and brother.

That led to the experience that changed Temple's life. Ben's sister Ann and her husband owned a ranch in Arizona. Temple went to stay with Aunt Ann for summer vacations.

Temple enjoyed life on the ranch. She liked solving problems. For instance, Aunt Ann's cattle kept wandering onto other people's property. Temple designed a gate that would close on its own to keep them inside. She was happy to have accomplished her goal—only to realize that she had created a new problem when she couldn't make the gate open wide enough for cars and trucks to drive through. She almost gave up. After seeing how the air vents opened and closed at her aunt's house, though, she copied their design, using a handle and pulleys to make the gate work!

The cows inspired Temple to solve her own problems too. When it was time to give the cows their vaccinations, they would go into a squeeze chute. Temple noticed that the cows became calm when the side panels of the chute pressed against them. Several days later, she had a panic attack. She asked Aunt Ann to let her into the squeeze chute. Her aunt pressed the sides of the chute against her. She later wrote, "I felt a wave of relaxation . . . For about an hour afterward I felt very calm and serene."

If Temple hated other people hugging her, why did she like the pressure of the squeeze chute? She said it was because she could control it herself. Other people hugging her frightened her and made her want to scream and run away.

When she returned to boarding school in the fall, she decided to build a squeeze machine to help her calm down. Her classmates laughed at her. The headmaster called her mother, and together they tried to prevent Temple from making this contraption. They said the other students would

think she was weird and not want to be friends with her.

Temple persisted. She knew what was best for herself. Her science teacher, William Carlock, encouraged her. He said this project could be an experiment for his class. The headmaster and Temple's mother gave in. Temple built her own squeeze machine and was able to use it to help keep herself calm when she needed it. Later, Temple added padding and better control levers to make the squeeze machine more comfortable and easier to use.

The boarding school also had a stable with horses the students could ride. Temple loved spending time with the horses. Some of them also had behavioral problems because of the way they'd been treated before they came to the school. Temple took

good care of the horses. She cleaned their stalls and brushed and petted them. She felt that she and the horses had a lot in common.

When Temple got into trouble with her classmates or didn't hand in assignments, her punishment was that she couldn't ride or even visit the horses. This gave her a reason to work hard and not get into fights with the other students.

She graduated from boarding school with good grades and got into Franklin Pierce College, a small college nearby.

Even though she'd lived away from home, Temple was nervous about going to college. She would have to leave her favorite teacher, Mr. Carlock. He said she could visit him whenever she wanted. He told her to think about going to a new place as going through a door.

Temple liked that image of a door. She learned by "thinking in pictures," each problem a picture in her mind. That's how she could see the air vent lever at Aunt Ann's ranch and create the same kind of lever for the self-closing gate. At boarding school she used to climb to the top of the stairs and open the trapdoor to the roof so she could see everything below in the moonlight.

Being able to see things from afar made her calm. "I was like an animal surveying the plains for lions," she said.

Temple kept this image of a door in her mind and the squeeze machine next to her bed. With the support of her mother and her favorite teacher, she was ready for the next stage in her life!

CHAPTER 3

Through the Back Door

Temple studied psychology at college because she wanted to understand how the mind works. She thought she'd learn more about herself and about other people whose words and behavior often confused her. For instance, she hated parties. They were noisy and crowded. She couldn't hear what other people were saying, and sweaty people would stand too close to her—or try to hug her!

Other students liked parties best of all. Living

in the dorm among them was like being "an anthro-pologist on Mars," as she later told the famous doctor and writer Oliver Sacks. Because anthro-pologists study societies, or groups of people, that are different from their own, this was a perfect description for Temple's experience in college. The student dorm served as a laboratory where she could observe how other young people lived and behaved. This skill of observing people alone and in groups would help her greatly in her work with animals.

Temple got top grades in science, history, and English classes, but she barely passed math and French. She failed the math part of the test to get into graduate school but convinced the animal sci-ence department at Arizona State University to accept her anyway. "I had to get through school by going through the back door," she wrote later on.

Temple found math challenging, but even more challenging was being a woman in the field of animal science. Some of her professors and the ranchers she did research with didn't think women should be animal scientists. Ranchers, managers at meatpacking plants, and other students played mean tricks on her. To gross her out and scare her away, they took her to a blood pit, which contained the waste from cattle that had been slaughtered to produce meat. Temple wasn't scared, but she was angry. She wanted to teach those men a lesson! She stepped into the pit, stomped her feet, and kicked blood onto the manager. After that, they realized they weren't going to get rid of her. Temple was there to stay.

Temple studied many things: the design of

the squeeze chute for vaccinations, the dipping vat
to kill insects on cattle hides, and the chute that
herded cattle and other animals to be slaughtered.
She liked studying animals because she believed
she and they shared many of the same feelings

and fears. Like them, she was easily frightened by flashing lights, loud noises, and change.

Because Temple thought in pictures, she saw the places and situations that upset the animals. She would walk the path the cattle walked, looking out at their eye level, and see things that caused them to panic: sunbeams reflecting from a metal grate or a shirt hanging from a fence. She had been drawing plans for inventions ever since she was in high school. Now she drew plans for the enclosures she imagined, ones that would make cattle calmer as they moved from place to place.

She noticed that cattle liked to walk in circles. Most chutes had sharp angles and turns. She designed a circular chute and tried to convince the ranchers and meat-processing companies to build this new chute. Even though it cost more money, too many animals were getting hurt the old way.

When cattle become bruised, their meat has gristle and cannot be sold. Frightened, unhappy cattle produce meat that is less tender and tasty. The ranchers and meat-processing plants were losing money by not redesigning their chutes.

When they told her no, Temple persisted. She came up with another way of going through the back door. She would write articles for magazines about her ideas!

Temple improved her writing so her articles could help change people's minds. She published dozens of articles in magazines for livestock handling, animal behavior, and engineering.

Ranchers and managers of meat-processing companies took notice of this curious woman with interesting ideas. A company that built livestock-handling facilities, Corral Industries, offered her a job. They wanted to use her ideas for the corrals and chutes that they built for meatpacking plants.

Temple didn't like to travel to unfamiliar places or have her schedule change. But after meat-packing plants asked her to design their chutes, she got used to it. She grew more confident about speaking in public. Her articles and her redesigned

chutes led to lectures and a steady job as a professor of animal science at Colorado State University.

When she gave advice to livestock companies, they would give her hats to show their appreciation of her work. When she spoke at conferences, she would save her badges. She enjoyed showing visitors her giant collection of hats and badges.

Today, more than one-third of all US livestock-handling facilities are based on Temple Grandin's designs. By persisting and going through the back door, Temple now stands at the front door of her profession!

·····························

CHAPTER 4

A Decent Life for the Animals

Along with curved chutes to move cattle, Temple designed a device to hold cattle in place when they reach the slaughterhouse. It was based on the squeeze chute, but with a conveyer belt under the animal's body. Temple wanted the cattle to feel calm before they were killed instantly and painlessly by a bolt to the head.

It made Temple sad to know that the animals she'd worked with would be killed for food. She

said she "wept and wept" when she finished her study of pigs for her doctorate in animal science and she had to slaughter the pigs to examine their brains. For months, she observed how pigs played with straw and other objects and became smarter and happier when they had more "toys" to play with.

If Temple cared so much about these animals

and their happiness, why did she work with companies that slaughtered the animals?

Temple observed that humans need other animals for food: "The fact that humans evolved as both plant and meat eaters means that the vast majority of human beings are going to continue to eat both. Humans are animals, too, and we do what our animal natures tell us to do."

At the same time, Temple believed, "We owe [the animals] a decent life and a decent death, and their lives should be as low-stress as possible." Animals raised for food, such as cattle and pigs, would not have been born in the first place if humans didn't use them for that purpose. They would have no life at all. Temple believed that animals should enjoy their lives before they are eaten. They should live in herds the way they are meant to live and be protected from anything that might hurt or frighten them. That means their living conditions should be clean, they should be well-fed, and anyone who comes in contact with them should treat them with kindness and respect.

Temple observed that as animals go to slaughter, they don't know what's going to happen. They cannot see into the future. They only want to avoid pain. With her understanding of their needs and feelings, Temple made it possible for cattle, pigs, chickens, and other animals used for food to die feeling much less pain and fear. She said that a well-run meat-processing facility is "more humane than nature." In nature, many animals starve or freeze to death, or are chased long distances and captured by other, bigger animals. On well-run farms and ranches, it's possible for them to live good lives.

In the late 1990s, McDonald's hired Temple to create checklists and to inspect its facilities for handling beef, pork, and chicken. Wendy's and Burger King soon followed. Today, more and more meat plants are using Temple's checklists for the humane treatment of animals, and conditions are improving.

Other places came calling. Temple began consulting with owners of dogs and horses whose animals had behavioral problems. Zoos hired her to make sure their animals on display were healthy and happy. One of the biggest problems with zoo animals is boredom, because they don't have the varied environments found in nature. Temple recommended ways to keep animals active and interested without causing them to panic at the new things zookeepers introduced.

Temple had another good effect on the live-stock industry. When she started out, she was one of the only women working in animal science. She urged companies to hire women to handle the animals. Through her observations, she believed, "[women handlers] are gentler than all-guy groups and they keep the facility cleaner." Today, ranches and stockyards are full of women handlers.

Temple became a role model, a teacher, and a supporter of other women entering the field of animal science. Because of her efforts, women enjoy greater opportunities, and the animals benefit too!

....

Learning About Autism

When Temple started traveling all over the United States to design enclosures and give advice on the handling of livestock, she noticed something that worried her a lot. The states where farm animals lived in the worst conditions were also the states where people with disabilities suffered from prejudice, isolation, and cruel treatment.

Temple knew that she could have been torn

away from her family and sent to a home for disabled children. She could have been mistreated there. She knew how lucky she was. Her family had a lot of money, and her mother refused to give up on her. Her teachers encouraged her to pursue her interests and invent things like the squeeze machine.

Now that she had become a respected scientist and university professor, Temple wanted to help other autistic people achieve their dreams. To do this, she first had to tell the world that she was autistic.

This was a scary decision for Temple. In the early 1980s, an autism diagnosis was a source of shame for many families. Some doctors blamed the mother for not showing enough affection. Most assumed autistic children would never grow up to live on their own or have jobs. Books, TV, and movies showed autistic people living in mental institutions.

If Temple talked about her autism diagnosis, maybe companies wouldn't want to hire her any-more. After all, her first job at Corral Industries had ended because she got into "social hassles," which was a polite way of saying that she hadn't gotten along well with the other people she worked with. As a designer with Corral Industries, she sent a letter to the president of a meatpacking com-pany describing every mistake the workers made in installing the equipment she had designed. He com-plained to her boss, who told her how disappointed he was with her. She quit that job soon after.

Yet Temple knew that telling the truth about her autism—just like telling the truth about badly installed equipment that could have injured the animals—was more important. If she lost jobs because of it, she would find better ones.

Again, she started by writing articles for magazines. In 1986, she published her life story in a book titled *Emergence: Labeled Autistic*. She shocked many psychologists, including the

famous doctor Oliver Sacks. He hadn't thought that an autistic person was capable of writing an autobiography. He wrote, "The autistic mind, it was supposed at that time, was incapable of self-understanding and understanding others . . ." Over the next few years, Temple convinced Dr. Sacks that he was wrong, and they became close friends.

Temple also found out that she could be wrong about autism. Like her friend Dr. Sacks, she learned her lesson and admitted her mistakes. In her 1995 book *Thinking in Pictures*, she wrote: "I translate both spoken and written words into full-color movies, complete with sound." At the time, she believed all autistic people thought in pictures as she did.

She soon discovered that "what's in *my* autistic brain is not necessarily what's in *someone else's* autistic brain." She found this out when she met with autistic children, their parents, and autistic adults. They told her they didn't think in photographs or movies. They couldn't draw detailed pictures from their imaginations. She listened to their stories and changed her way of thinking.

While Temple excelled at geometry, with its shapes and angles, some of the autistic people she met did better in algebra. Algebra is a type of math that uses patterns to solve problems, and Temple learned that many autistic people are great at recognizing the patterns of individual details. They are very good at math, solving puzzles, and playing chess.

She learned that some other autistic people do really well with language. They can organize

their thoughts into words and write entire books from outlines in their heads. They are skilled at memorizing facts and are often very interested in history.

Published in 2013, Temple's book *The Autistic Brain* described the different strengths of autistic people—those who think in pictures, in patterns, and in words. Like all good scientists, she used new information to change her beliefs about autism. In the process, she showed us how the world needs all kinds of autistic minds!

· ·

Different, Not Less

W hen she started writing about autism, Temple wanted to learn even more about herself and other autistic people. In the late 1980s, brain scans were a new technology. The big, noisy machines may have seemed scary, but Temple's curiosity outweighed her fear. She went for a brain scan and was glad that she did.

"Since then, every time a new scanning

method becomes available, I am the first in line to try it out," she wrote.

She also signed up for genetic tests, which are tests that look at the building blocks of a person that are inherited from their parents, to find out if autism runs in families. Today, most scientists believe it is genetic. As a result, they no longer blame the mother for the way she interacts with her baby, like they did when Temple was young. In addition, scientists have come to see that autism is a spectrum, with different people's autism impacting them in different ways. Autistic people's ability to speak and understand language can vary widely, and so can their interests and strengths.

Through her books, speeches at conferences, teaching, and consulting, Temple gave advice to parents, teachers, and autistic people themselves—the same way she gave advice to people who worked with animals. She became an expert in two different scientific fields!

It made Temple sad to see other autistic people not achieve their potential the way she had. She wanted autistic children to get the best education, one that built on their interests and strengths. She said teachers should encourage students to pursue the topics that fascinate them because they naturally learn reading, writing, and math in the process. Temple advised autistic children to find classmates with interests in common. That was how she made friends in high school and college and, later on, through her work. Most of her friends were other scientists or people who cared for animals.

Temple also helped autistic adults to find their

way in the world. She believed that society loses out when autistic people don't have jobs. When they work together, one person's strengths make up for another person's weaknesses. For example, Temple worked with professional writers on her books. Her ideas came to her in the form of pictures "clumped here and there." Her co-authors provided structure. She provided "the quick associations, the long-term memory, and the focus on details."

In her public speaking and meetings with

other autistic people, she advised persistence and trying new approaches—going through the back door—if others didn't understand or agree. "When you're a weird geek, you've got to learn to sell your work," she said.

Temple has used the phrase "different, not less," to describe autism. Because autistic people think differently, they can find solutions to problems that have stumped everyone else . . . or that other people haven't even realized are problems!

Temple has encouraged autistic people to be proud of who they are. It angered her when people talked about "curing" or "eliminating" autism. She said, "If I could snap my fingers and be nonautistic, I would not. Autism is part of who I am." If autism didn't exist, many things that make our lives easier would not have been invented. Society would not have advanced as far as it has today. "Without autism traits, we might still be living in caves," she once wrote.

Temple's advice for autistic people is good advice for everyone. Everyone has ideas and ways of seeing the world that are different. Everyone runs into obstacles. The most important thing is to believe in those ideas, make them the best they can be, and persist.

Different, not less. Throughout her life, Temple has demonstrated both creativity and courage. She's used her difference—autism—to become a leader in two fields. In the process, she has showed what we all can do when we embrace our own differences and those of others!

HOW YOU CAN PERSIST

by *Lyn Miller-Lachmann*

To honor Temple Grandin's creativity and courage, here are some activities you can do by yourself or with friends and family:

1. Observe an animal as it goes about its day. This can be your pet or an animal you see in nature. What makes the animal curious? What frightens the

animal? What does the animal like to eat? Does it have "toys" it likes to play with?

2. Imagine you're the caretaker of an imaginary animal, like a dragon or a unicorn. Make a list of things you would need to do to keep the animal happy and safe, and to keep the people around that animal happy and safe. (This is similar to an assignment that Temple gives to her students at Colorado State University.)

3. Invent a toy or design a home for your imaginary animal and make or build it.

4. Keep a journal of things that make you nervous or frightened. Make a list of things that you do to calm down.

Share your list with a friend or family member.

5. Think of someone in your class who is different from you. Make a list of things you're good at doing and things that person is good at doing. Get involved in a project or activity where your abilities and the other person's abilities work together to get things done.

6. Research other autistic people who have made a difference in the world.

7. Read a book by an autistic author.

Acknowledgments

....

I would like to thank my agent, Jacqui Lipton, and my editors, Talia Benamy and Jill Santopolo. It is an honor and a privilege to work with such a talented team. This opportunity would not have been possible without the original PerSisterhood: Chelsea Clinton, Alexandra Boiger, Gillian Flint, and the production team at Philomel. Finally, I thank my daughter, Madeleine, for her advice on this book and for her dedication to her own students.

ᴄ References ᴐ

BOOKS AND ARTICLES:

Grandin, Temple, and Catherine Johnson.
Animals in Translation: Using the Mysteries of Autism to Decode Animal Behavior. New York: Scribner, 2005.

Grandin, Temple, and Catherine Johnson.
Animals Make Us Human: Creating the Best Life for Animals. Boston: Houghton Mifflin Harcourt, 2009.

Grandin, Temple, and Richard Panek. *The Autistic Brain: Thinking Across the Spectrum.* Boston: Houghton Mifflin Harcourt, 2013.

Grandin, Temple, with Betsy Lerner. *Calling All Minds: How to Think and Create Like an Inventor.* New York: Philomel, 2018.

Grandin, Temple. *Thinking in Pictures: And Other Reports from My Life with Autism.* Second edition. New York: Vintage, 2006.

Miller-Lachmann, Lyn. "On Meeting Temple Grandin." The Pirate Tree: Social Justice and Children's Literature. July 25, 2013. thepiratetree.com/2013/07/25/on-meeting-temple-grandin. Retrieved December 30, 2020.

Sacks, Oliver. "An Anthropologist on Mars."
New Yorker. December 27, 1993. newyorker.com
/magazine/1993/12/27/anthropologist-mars.
Retrieved November 19, 2020.

Seidel, Jeff. "Betting on hope: Mother of an
autistic college professor reaches out to other
autistic parents. *Detroit Free Press.* April 3,
2009. catholic.org/news/hf/faith/story
.php?id=33003. Retrieved December 30,
2020.

Silberman, Steve. *NeuroTribes: the Legacy of
Autism and the Future of Neurodiversity.*
New York: Avery, 2015.

FURTHER READING/VIEWING:

Guglielmo, Amy, Jacqueline Tourville, and Giselle Potter (illus.). *How to Build a Hug: Temple Grandin and Her Amazing Squeeze Machine.* New York: Atheneum, 2018.

McCully, Emily Arnold. "Temple Grandin." In *She Did It! 21 Women Who Changed the Way We Think* (pp. 237–246). New York: Disney/ Hyperion, 2018.

Mosca, Julia Finley, and Daniel Rieley (illus.). *The Girl Who Thought in Pictures: The Story of Dr. Temple Grandin.* Seattle: The Innovation Press, 2017.

Temple Grandin (TV movie). Directed by Mick Jackson, performances by Claire Danes, Julia Ormond, David Strathairn. HBO, 2010.

LYN MILLER-LACHMANN grew up in Texas before leaving to attend Princeton University. She has a master's in library and information science from the University of Wisconsin, Madison, and a master of fine arts in writing for children and young adults from Vermont College of Fine Arts. She's taught middle school students in a variety of subjects and is the author of *Rogue*, *Surviving Santiago*, *Gringolandia*, and *Once Upon a Cuento*. Her books often feature characters on the autism spectrum, just like Lyn herself. Lyn and her husband split their time between New York and Lisbon, Portugal.

Photo credit: Don Whipple

You can visit Lyn online at
lynmillerlachmann.com
or follow her on Twitter
@lmillerlachmann
and on Instagram
@lynmillerlachmann

GILLIAN FLINT has worked as a professional illustrator since earning an animation and illustration degree in 2003. Her work has since been published in the UK, USA and Australia. In her spare time, Gillian enjoys reading, spending time with her family and puttering about in the garden on sunny days. She lives in the northwest of England.

You can visit Gillian Flint online at
gillianflint.com
or follow her on Twitter
@GillianFlint
and on Instagram
@gillianflint_illustration

CHELSEA CLINTON is the author of the #1 *New York Times* bestseller *She Persisted: 13 American Women Who Changed the World*; *She Persisted Around the World: 13 Women Who Changed History*; *She Persisted in Sports: American Olympians Who Changed the Game*; *Don't Let Them Disappear: 12 Endangered Species Across the Globe*; *It's Your World: Get Informed, Get Inspired & Get Going!*; *Start Now!: You Can Make a Difference*; with Hillary Clinton, *Grandma's Gardens* and *Gutsy Women*; and, with Devi Sridhar, *Governing Global Health: Who Runs the World and Why?* She is also the Vice Chair of the Clinton Foundation, where she works on many initiatives, including those that help empower the next generation of leaders. She lives in New York City with her husband, Marc, their children and their dog, Soren.

Courtesy of the author

You can follow Chelsea Clinton on Twitter
@ChelseaClinton
or on Facebook at
facebook.com/chelseaclinton

ALEXANDRA BOIGER has illustrated nearly twenty picture books, including the She Persisted books by Chelsea Clinton; the popular Tallulah series by Marilyn Singer; and the Max and Marla books, which she also wrote. Originally from Munich, Germany, she now lives outside of San Francisco, California, with her husband, Andrea, daughter, Vanessa, and two cats, Luiso and Winter.

Photo credit: Vanessa Blasich

You can visit Alexandra Boiger online at
alexandraboiger.com
or follow her on Instagram
@alexandra_boiger

Read about more inspiring women in the

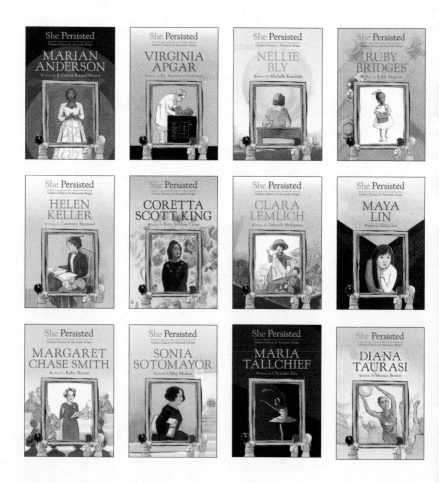

She Persisted series!